All in the Same Boat

NOTES FROM A MIND THAT WANDERS

All in the Same Boat

NOTES FROM A MIND THAT WANDERS

Marcia J. Monbleau

Cover & Illustrations
by
Lucretia Romey

I'm thankful
for Pat and Lucretia and Kevin, who read and drew and helped build this, and for the best people and good days at *TCC*. Old times there are not forgotten.

Bog House Press
Harwich Port,
Massachusetts

First Printing

ISBN 0-9676220-2-6

In memory
of my parents,
Charles & Lola Monbleau,
and brothers,
David and Milton

and
for
my sister, Nancy,
who I have now (just) forgiven
for making me sit at the faucet end of the bathtub
when we were little.

Contents

Cranky Yankee

Local Color

Foreword

Writing a book is easier than writing an introduction to it. When you write, you just keep going. But when all is said and done, you must stand back and try to figure out what the thing is.

In this case, it is not a novel, a history or mystery, a self-help or how-to book, biography, collection of verse or cookbook.

What then?

"Travel diary" might be a possible description, because I do believe we're all in the same boat—a boat that is going somewhere or other almost all of the time.

But the more I think about it, the more I lean toward an old New England tradition.

So I shall call it "hash."

To make hash, you take something that's already in the refrigerator—leftover roast beef, corned beef, lamb—and grind it up. Then cook potatoes, carrots and such, add them to the meat and put the whole mess into a frying pan.

I worked at a newspaper for quite a long time, and

together with normal reporting and editorial duties there, I wrote anything that occurred to me—in a column that appeared whenever the muse either whispered or hollered. I'll always be grateful for that privilege.

Our editor and publisher—a man who meant a lot to a lot of us for a lot of years—had a rule. If, after our work appeared in the paper, we had a chance to sell it elsewhere, that was fine with him. Such opportunities, he said with a growl, might help compensate for the puny salaries he paid. I never took him up on that offer—until now.

So along with new ingredients are some others that have been in the refrigerator, so to speak.

This book is about life—about things, events, places and people that have made me happy, unhappy, puzzled, crabby or nostalgic. If this boat notion is correct, perhaps readers will feel the same way.

It's my boat, but there are plenty of seats. If you've got time and want to ride along, come aboard.

But sit down fast, so we don't tip over.

MJM
Winter 2004

Home & Hearth

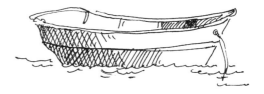

❖

It Never Snows on Cape Cod

Dear Summer Friend,

Your favorite parking space at the beach is available today. I thought about you when I drove by, and I remembered us hopping from car shadow to car shadow to avoid burning our bare feet.

There's three feet of snow there now.

Do you have trouble picturing that? Have you ever been here when it wasn't sun and ice cream or gin and tonic on a warm evening porch?

I'll tell you about the other day, if you have a minute. Imagine this.

It began sometime after midnight. I woke up and knew it was happening, because of the silence. Rain is noisy. No-rain is quiet. But the quietest of all is the white-muffled, feather-pillow quiet of snowfall.

And this was to be no dainty dusting. By my 7 o'clock early-morning dog-out, the air was thick and swirling and the driveway—75 feet long on the straightaway— looked like a landing strip.

Back in the kitchen, I kicked off low boots, poured coffee and listened to the radio man. He said the roads were a mess, and if people would just stay put for awhile highway crews could get to work.

As it turned out, that would have been the last chance to make a run for it. The sky sat right down on us. The wind drew circles in the drifts and my birdbath disappeared.

I know what you're saying; in most places a vanishing birdbath is a "so what?" But around here they don't get buried every day of the week. Housebound, I stood looking out the back window. Measuring. Gauging. Going, going, gone the birdbath.

This was serious. I pulled on higher boots and went outside again. By now the world was done up in a set of no-colors, included among them white, tree trunk-brown and soaked-shingle gray. And the dog, assuming correctly that white is white is white, piddled on the deck, rather than walking all the way to the yard. In her shoes—which, of course, she wasn't wearing—I'd have done the same.

I hiked out to the still-unplowed road. Amy followed—enthusiastic, if short-legged—hurling herself from one of my bootprints into the next. I looked up and down the road into white mushy silence and then back toward the house, where everything I'd ever planted had gone the way of the birdbath. No azaleas. Junipers bent low and mounded over. Window boxes capped with snow-cones. And to the right of the driveway, day-after-day-after-daylilies lay deep down and hibernating.

By now I was wrapped in wet white. My boots were only half as high as they needed to be, and I was missing a dog. She was there, trying to hide on the windless side of a pine tree. Black eyelashes sparkled with ice, and a gumdrop of snow sat on her nose.

Time to go inside, where I held a yardstick to the snowline on my slacks. Thirty inches.

Another world took over then. Warm and closed in—with boot puddles and wet-wool smell. And the television. And the phone. Those worked. And food. Driving snow attached itself to every side of the house—insulating—packing—covering windows. By mid-afternoon, I was sealed off in my snow hut, without sound, without sight.

Some of us maintained voice contact throughout the day, comparing conditions, complaints, levels of inactivity and junk food fantasies.

"The snow in my yard is up to the third step!"

"Oh yeah? Well, my birdbath is covered!"

"Really?"

"Yeah."

"What are you eating? I can hear you eating."

"Carrot sticks."

"Liar."

At one house, a friend was painting a wall cabinet and making grilled cheese sandwiches. Her kids, in some kind of no-school, snow-induced frenzy, kept going out dry and coming in wet, so the clothes dryer went full tilt all day.

Another friend thought she'd "better use up" a package of Nestle's Chocolate Bits, which is the sneakiest way I'd ever heard that put.

And I, having had the foresight to tape "An Affair to Remember," curled up on the floor, sniffled with Cary and Deborah and tried to ignore the sirens' wail of the Duncan Hines Brownie mix in the cupboard.

Nicky (Cary) finally saw the painting and realized that Terry (Deborah) had tried to get to the Empire State Building, so that all worked out well. And as the no-sun went down, I bundled up again, grabbed the shovel, leaned into the snow and made one more effort to maintain the path I'd cleared between the house and shed. This was a grave error in judgment. As I headed back inside, my chiropractor's face—like Marley's ghost—grinned at me from the door knocker.

Just before midnight, I gathered up the little creature

who had spent the entire day in someone else's footprints and—carrying her—trudged out to the mostly-plowed road.

There, in the nightclub-pink glow of a sodium vapour streetlight, she performed a long-pent-up, racing, spinning dance to freedom.

The snow had stopped, and our world—one you wouldn't recognize—was smooth, heaped high, frozen-magic white—save for a black speck of spaniel.

It was beyond silence, and we were the only two in it. Of course, it won't be that way when you get back.

You'll just have to imagine.

Measuring by the Yard

Every now and then I hear of someone who's moved into a condominium or an apartment here or over the bridge. They're glad to be rid of maintenance worries, and even happier to quit doing yard work.

They leave behind rakes and shovels, hoes, twisted hoses, bug spray, part bags of fertilizer, lime and bone meal. They leave behind snow shovels and rock salt, birdbaths, cement frogs and plastic plant hangers.

How nice for them.

Someday—maybe—but for me and for now, I'm not turning in my trowel.

Nobody who comes by would think for a minute that professionals are at work here, designing or planting, feeding or weeding. Flowers and shrubs are strangely placed and oddly spaced. There are tall things in front of short things, things that grow wildly and things that are hanging on for dear life, looking feeble and straggly.

I stuck a stick of pussywillow in the ground three years ago, and it's now a 14-foot high tree-thing. Thirty tulip bulbs planted in '99 obviously fell clear through to China and haven't been seen since. Of a dozen "perennial" chrysanthemums planted, most disappeared forever, and one that always comes back is the size of a Volkswagen.

Money Plant spreads like wildfire, yews reach up and grab onto the house and hostas flourish, but a few rhododendrons look like they were dragged kicking and screaming across Death Valley, and the condition of the lavender is very disturbing.

I've put shade-loving plants in the sun and sun-loving plants in the shade. Annually, I forget where the perennials are. I forget to cut back the Buddleia bushes when you're supposed to, and I'm not sure which parts of hydrangeas should be pruned in the spring. Or is it the fall?

A hardy clump of something-or-other comes up by the kitchen door every spring. It may be from the weed family, but it's quite pretty and people ask about it frequently. I decided to call it "Purple Lapidalia." When someone asks, "What's that?" I say, "Purple Lapidalia" in an authoritative voice, and they repeat the name a few times so they can go ask for it someplace. That should be fun.

I've seen yards where spring-to-fall color never stops. Shrubs and flowers come to life in orderly fashion. Blossoming continues through the season, tall plants are background to short ones, colors complement one another, borders are handsomely edged, nothing ever droops, drops or gets spindly and there is not a weed to be seen.

I have no idea how that happens.

I'm pretty content to sit on my rump and dig holes. When a small green thing starts poking through the dirt in spring, the fact that I have absolutely no idea what I planted makes the event an annual surprise party. When the small green thing gets to identification size, I can dance around it singing, "You're a hyacinth!"

If I had a philosophy—which I don't—it probably would be this: I've invited these wonderful things into the yard, planted, watered and given them some food. I leave it to them to be what they are and to know what they're doing.

And if it's not all perfect and planned and arranged according to height, color and blooming time, so what? Every once in awhile, it's so pretty it makes me dizzy.

The Breck's catalogue order arrived today. I got seven kinds of bulbs. At the moment, I don't remember what they are.

But I have to dig 180 holes before the ground freezes.

Home Uninsurance

This is about a squirrel, but it begins with a dog and ends with an insurance man.

It was a dark and stormy night when the dog flung herself at the door to a closed-off room and started a barking racket that could be heard around town.

Average, mid-size dogs don't say "woof, woof," when you really stop to listen. It's more like "Arrh, arrh, ARRHH!" Then they take a breath and repeat "Arrh, arrh, ARRH!" If they're really agitated, they skip the breathing altogether, so it's "Arrh, arrh, arrh, arrh, arrh" until your teeth rattle.

Well, that's what happened.

The door to the room was closed because it was winter and because there is "low-cost electric heat" in there—an oxymoron if there ever was one.

But when a dog starts "arrh-arrh"ing at the closed door to a dark room, well, anyone would get jumpy. A familiar, cozy and secure home becomes a strange and evil place where things just might go "slash" and "rip" in the night.

I opened the door, and Killer Cocker flew past into the pitch black. "Arrh, arrh, ARRH!" As I turned on lights, the room became its happy self and I could not see one single axe murderer.

Nor could the dog. She sniffed the middle, the corners and as far up the walls as her nose would reach. The volume of her voice dropped to "Ummph, ummph," then to a soft clucking in her throat, the way dogs do when they want to have the last word.

Everything was fine. I turned off lights and closed the door, and all was peace once more.

At 4 o'clock the following afternoon, I went to fetch something from the same room. I picked it up, turned to leave and then did one of those movie double-takes. Something was most definitely amiss.

Slowly, I turned. The room had been attacked.

There were pieces of wood everywhere. Drapes had been pulled down and shredded, curtain rods ripped from their brackets, sofa pillows scattered and torn.

I moved toward the windows, stunned into slow motion. The sills were eaten away, the mullions chomped all the way to to the glass.

I backed out, closed the door and turned to see the dog, smiling at me, with an I-told-you-so twinkle in her eyes. She thought I was an idiot.

Something was in that room. Something monstrous— with teeth and claws and a chain-saw. I tiptoed back in, opened the door to the yard—and left, hoping whatever IT was would leave on its own.

I then did what anyone who pays for homeowners' insurance would do. I called for help and was told that an adjuster would be over the next morning.

He was. And he was very sympathetic. He looked at the ruined drapes, the wrecked windows, and said "Tsk, tsk" quite a lot.

"This is really something," he said, shaking his head. I agreed, shaking mine.

He got down on his hands and knees and looked

12

under a table. "Uh-oh," he said, poking at something on the floor.

Here is a warning for homeowners: When an insurance adjuster says, "Uh-oh," you are not going to be happy.

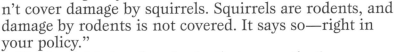

"Uh-oh," he said again, picking up something and holding it up for me to see.

"Squirrel droppings," he said. "A squirrel must have fallen down the chimney and did all this trying to get out."

"Wow," I said.

"That's too bad," he said. "Your policy doesn't cover damage by squirrels. Squirrels are rodents, and damage by rodents is not covered. It says so—right in your policy."

He shook his head again, in that sympathetic way. "Now if these had been raccoon droppings, you'd be covered. But not for squirrel droppings."

Some time later, after five windows and pairs of drapes had been replaced, I decided I would get a coffee can and go out looking for raccoon droppings—for possible future use.

Before I could do that, however, a letter arrived from the insurance company, notifying all policy holders that damage by raccoons would no longer be covered.

I've gotten a bigger can now and am on the lookout for buffalo poop.

Stuff & Nonsense

With rain splunking on the roof and no sign of a let-up, it was a heads or tails sort of day. Heads, I could curl up around a book and eat Mallomars all afternoon. Tails, I could hunker down and clean out the desk in the kitchen.

Because cleanliness is next to Godliness, and trimming fat thighs is next to impossible, I rolled up imaginary sleeves and approached the old piece of furniture with some trepidation.

The desk is not your average sort, with a flat surface and one slim drawer. It's the type a type like me should not own—of schoolmaster design, with two shelves on either side and a lift-up top that conceals a great, yawning pit where Stuff collects and multiplies. If I drop two buttons in, they have baby buttons.

The lift-top is a breeze for pack rats. Left hand raises lid. Right hand shoots stuff inside, while left hand lowers lid slowly. Lift. Shoot. Lower. One, two, three.

The deep shelves on the right house canned goods. There are books on the left side, and my first chore is to empty that area until the puppy learns to mind her own business. She keeps taking paperbacks into the living room.

Now to the heart of the matter. Keepies will go on a

TV tray to my left; tossies will be pitched into the tall wastebasket on my right.

Lift top, lean it back against wall and begin.

What's in there?

A yellowing note to myself containing some possible song lyrics, which, upon closer examination, are beyond awful.

A fly swatter with gunk on it. (That goes into the sink to be rinsed.) Some waterproof matches from the last time I went camping—at California's Mt. Whitney—in 1980—where I discovered that sleeping in my clothes on damp rocks is not my idea of a swell time.

A wrinkly map of Bermuda, seven expired coffee coupons, a large roll of masking tape, the gloves I couldn't find last winter, a 1993 Hallmark datebook and a microphone that plugs into heaven-knows-what.

An old pocket knife that says "Motorola" on it, a tin cream skimmer, a Mickey Mouse decal and three stones that were very, very important because I picked them up in—hmmm—some-place.

A letter from a friend in California telling me about her new house. (She has since gotten divorced and moved twice.) A dog comb. A dog brush. An ashtray that jumped into my pocket at the Golden Horseshoe Casino in Las Vegas.

An oak hand mirror, waiting to be refinished. An oval frame, waiting for an oval picture. A movie film from a trip to Barbados, waiting to be developed. A pitchpipe, a lifeguard's whistle and a purple kazoo.

One package of 24-inch shoelaces. Earmuffs, a recipe for "Magic Cookie Bars," 23 shark's teeth from a Florida beach, a wall thermometer, yard sale price stickers and a packet of Di-Gel, whatever that is.

Five buttons—no two alike. A nifty switchblade from Tijuana. (I thought it might come in handy. It hasn't.) A large, round cloth patch that says, "I Sell Coca-Cola in Bottles," nine envelopes of photo negatives, one large pack of golf tees (to be used when caning a chair, which I haven't learned how to do yet), one carefully-wrapped-in-plastic piece of sheet music ("Where Did Robinson Crusoe Go with Friday on Saturday Night?") and a green water pistol.

Quite some time later, I put four things in the wastebasket, slid everything else back into the desk, grabbed the Mallowmars and went into the living room.

I asked the dog to bring me a book.

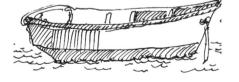

Feeling Squashed

It happened late last night.

I heard a muffled thump-thumping behind the house and then—nothing. Walking softly and carrying a big flower pot, I tiptoed across the dark kitchen, eased open the back door and stared into the fog that made even familiar things eery.

And then I saw it. "NO!" I screamed into the blackness. "Leave me alone! I can't take it anymore!"

Someone had been there. On the stoop was a small, plain basket, and inside it a ragged bit of cloth. Trembling, I reached down and plucked at the covering, turning it back until I saw THEM.

Twin zucchinis.

With tears flowing, I took the basket and went back inside, heading for the zucchini room which I'd built onto the house the previous August. Opening the door, I tossed in the twins, leaving them to make their own introductions.

It had begun innocently enough last year, as is so often the case with events that lead to terror. On the first Thursday in August, I had found in the mailbox a phone bill, a Publishers' Clearing House Sweepstakes offer, two letters and four zucchinis.

Three days later, I tripped over three more green things on my beach blanket. Two were left on the back seat of the car, and one had been wedged under the windshield wiper.

Someone, thinking to be clever, sprinkled a half-dozen of them throughout my garden, which didn't fool me as I was growing asters at the time.

When I was out watering the lawn one day, a long

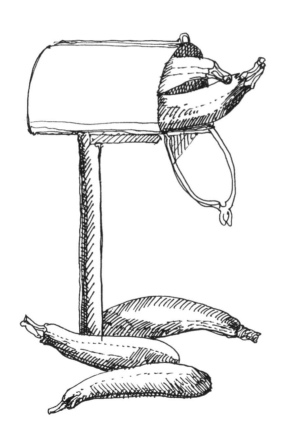

black sedan approached the house—slowly at first. Suddenly, the back door was flung open, a dozen zucchinis tossed out and the car sped away. I didn't get the license number. It was a professional job.

That's when I added on the room and began reading every cookbook I could lay my hands on.

It was easy at first. I had boiled, steamed or fried zucchini. Zucchini bread.

But I couldn't keep ahead. Still they came. One followed my dog home.

I had creamed zucchini, zucchini au vin, braised and mashed. I roasted it, poached it, baked and barbecued it. Escalloped. On toast. En brochette. Sliced with cream and sugar. Zucchini on a stick. Au gratin. Cakes, tarts, with marshmallow fluff, on coffee ice cream and between graham crackers.

But late in August, something even worse happened. I began to recognize them. I became attached. As individual personalities emerged, we spent more time together and stayed up late watching television.

I kept two of them—"Spot" and "Missy"—as pets, and sent the brightest one off to Finland on an exchange program. Veggie Jackson is playing on a farm team in Florida now, and Pucchini Zucchini is a freshman at the New England Conservatory of Music.

Shaking myself back to reality last night, I knew I couldn't go through it again. I won't eat them, and I can't afford any more tuition.

Saddest of all, at Spot's first birthday party last week, I noticed he's beginning to smell funny.

All Creatures Small & Smaller

The house got a little stuffy the other day. You know how it is when you've been indoors too long—paying bills, picking up, putting away, trying to figure out how spider webs that you whack away mid-morning are back in place by late afternoon—that sort of thing. Your head gets muzzy from breathing your own self-centered air.

This is a good time to go outside, check on the neighbors and see if there's anything you can do for them.

Mine seemed to be pretty content the other day.

When I went out the door, three bunnies froze in place. The rabbit theory is this, I'm sure: "If I stop breathing and don't move a whisker, she won't see me here four feet away." But I did, and they knew I did, and they eventually remembered that I'm the one who adds clover to the grass seed. So they started chewing again, and I moved on to see if any other neighbors were out and about.

The squirrel-proof bird feeders were working well, I thought. One squirrel hung by his toenails from a branch, emptying the feeder very nicely. Across the yard, another one climbed up a tree, launched itself at the feeder and knocked half the contents to the ground.

These rigs might better be called "bird-proof squirrel feeders."

I walked around, toeing in a dozen or so divots dug up by grubbing skunks the night before. A narrow, mounded line of grass curving across the yard showed where the voles were traveling underground to get from someplace to someplace else.

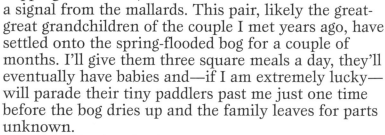

There was a soft flapping behind me, a signal from the mallards. This pair, likely the great-great grandchildren of the couple I met years ago, have settled onto the spring-flooded bog for a couple of months. I'll give them three square meals a day, they'll eventually have babies and—if I am extremely lucky— will parade their tiny paddlers past me just one time before the bog dries up and the family leaves for parts unknown.

Ground-feeding birds dropped down to finish off mallard leftovers, and the rabbits continued munching their way through supper.

In all, the neighbors seemed to be doing fine.

Politics

There Goes the Neighborhood

(Years ago, there were rumors that Richard M. Nixon was considering buying a house here. At the time, it seemed logical to make the best of a dubious situation.)

Dear Mr. Nixon,

I understand you are thinking of buying property in Harwich Port.

Have I got a deal for you!

A few years ago, I purchased a lovely half-acre on South Street, a tidy little road that winds through town from the Port to the Center. I should point out that South Street has four distinct sections: downtown (neat and convenient), the golf course (open and green), the elementary school block (extremely quiet, except for yellow buses twice daily) and mine, which is dominated by a handsome stand of green oil tanks.

The property itself is a sloping, easy to maintain parcel, dotted with scrub oak and unusual Cape Cod pines. These do not block the view because dead limbs have been lopped off to a height of approximately 30 feet.

I have converted the south portion of the front yard to a moss farm, and there is a handsome, yet maintenance-free area of bullbriars out back. The property is bordered on the west by a large ditch, former waterway to a near-by cranberry bog. This gully serves as a most convenient storage place for stumps, limbs, grass clippings and the many oak leaves that come with the property; it would mean a considerable savings to you, Mr. Nixon, because you would not need to purchase a dump sticker.

May I also point out that a previous owner buried several hundred pounds of cinder blocks at the northwest corner of the site, which would come in handy should you wish to putter around and do odd jobs. You might also enjoy digging up some of the many wine bottles there, some of which date as far back as the mid-1960s.

The house itself is a treasure, sir. It contains four rooms, a full bath (I would, of course, leave the shower curtain), crawl space and a handy attic storage area reached through one of those clever holes in the ceiling.

There is wall-to-wall carpeting throughout, with only a few teensy doggie marks.

The living room is spacious, and large sliding doors provide an unobstructed view of the ditch.

Because you probably are concerned about money-saving features, you will be pleased to know that a wood-stove has been installed in the fireplace. (We can make some arrangement about those soot marks on the ceiling.)

While the house gives the impression of being quite large, it is extremely practical. It is a three-plug home; that is to say, while you are vacuuming, Mr. Nixon, you need plug into only three outlets to clean the entire dwelling.

As if the house and grounds are not enough, there is a bonus feature here. I call it a "shed," although it has been called other things from time to time. Designed to look old, it has a sagging roofline and walls that lean ever so slightly. I have had three of those walls rebuilt, but should you be interested, the fourth wall is in its original condition and may be moved out to provide additional space for a horse or dirt bike. (This wall could be moved quite easily because—due to a slight rotting problem—the bottom of it no longer touches the ground.)

The district, I rush to add, is zoned to permit the keeping of chickens.

Mr. Nixon, I realize you are viewing property in the neighborhood of Saquatucket Harbor, but have you considered all the consequences of living in such an area? For example, there is a sign at the entrance to Saquatucket Bluffs which reads "Residents Only." That would discourage friends of yours from visiting, and certainly would keep cute little trick-or-treaters from stopping by in October.

Moreover, all sorts of riffraff would be going past your house in large yachts, and have you ever smelled a low tide, Mr. Nixon?

Perhaps most important, your home would not be convenient to the supermarket, Dairy Queen or Go-Kart Track.

I am most reluctant to sell, particularly because I have only 26 years left to go on my mortgage. But I am willing to sit down and discuss the possibility. I'm sure we could come to terms.

May I hear from you?

the Nixon years

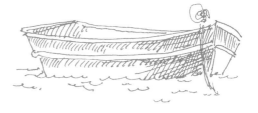

Nancy & The China Syndrome

Word is out that the First Lady has ordered some new First China to replace the old First China, which has been around since the Trumans held the lease. Folks in the White House have been making do with the same old dishes all these years, and that's a shame.

Mrs. Reagan has asked the Lenox people to come up with something simple, with a band around the edge and a cute little Presidential seal in the center.

I follow Mrs. Reagan's activities here with considerable interest because I, too, have been thinking of buying new dishes.

Many years ago, while browsing through a favorite place—the Pottery Shack in Laguna Beach, California—I came upon a set of ironstone that made my heart beat a little faster. But it was beyond my budget. The price for six place settings was $47.50, and I came home dishless.

But on a return visit a year later, there was a close-out sale, which made that trip worthwhile, let me tell you. I carried my $28 pottery home on the plane, along with a two-foot redwood roadrunner, paper flowers from Tijuana and a bottle of banana brandy.

As you might imagine, the years have taken their toll. There are chips, nicks, and one bowl has a serious crack.

31

I expect, some day soon, it will let go quietly, dumping granola and one per cent milk into my lap.

So, "Small world," I thought to myself as I read of Nancy's plans. "They're just folks, like the rest of us, and we all need a plate for our tuna noodle casserole."

But the Reagans have more friends than I do, because the First Lady is buying 220 place settings. I have six. Each setting of the new First China will cost $952. Mine ran about $4, plus change.

I noted one other minor difference.

Each White House place setting contains 18 pieces, some of which I've never heard of. I have a plate, a salad plate, bowl, cup and saucer. Period.

I use the big plate for big things and the little plate for small stuff. I know it's for salad, but a peanut butter sandwich fits, too, and so do scrambled eggs or leftover creamed chipped beef.

I put soup in the soup bowls, unless I want to put cereal there, and it seems to work well for ice cream or pudding or anything else that's wet. I don't use the cups much, because if you use a mug you don't have to wash

a saucer that isn't even dirty. I don't understand saucers, anyway. If you spill coffee into a saucer and then pick up the cup, there's coffee on the bottom and it drips onto your leg. On the other hand, if you spill from a mug, it just soaks into the tablecloth.

So I'd like to ask you, Mrs. Reagan, about your place setting, because it seems just a bit—umm—unnecessary.

You have a "dinner plate" and a "fish plate." Isn't fish "dinner?" Does the fish plate have a different shape— say, oval?—so the tail fits on? Maybe you could cut off the tail and head so fish will fit on a "dinner plate."

You have a "salad plate" and a "dessert plate." Can't you have your salad and then wash the plates in time for dessert?

Now tell me about the "soup plate," "bouillon cup" and "cream soup cup and stand." Soup is soup is soup, Mrs. Reagan. It's all wet and needs to go in a thing that holds wet stuff. Why does cream soup need a "stand?"

In the same category, you have a "berry bowl" and a "cereal bowl." Again, this is wet stuff that, if push comes to shove, would fit in a soup "plate." I don't think berries are fussy about things like that. My berries go wherever they're told.

A "butter plate." No need for that. I usually balance my butter on the edge of my "dinner plate" or on the "salad plate." In fact, you could go into the dining room and ask for a show of hands; "Who wants butter on their baked potato?" Then just smack it right on there before you leave the kitchen.

You have a "cocktail cup." Heaven only knows why you need that, when you already have a "cereal bowl," "berry bowl" and, I nearly forgot, a "finger bowl." Give each guest a wash-n-dry, and use the finger bowl for cereal. Or berries. Better yet, don't invite people who stick their fingers in the food.

The First China setting includes a "tea cup and saucer" and a "demitasse and saucer." Why not get some good mugs? Drop in a teabag, and it's a tea cup. You want demitasse? Fill it halfway. Mugs are good, too, for cream soup.

Finally, you have a "ramekin." What is that? I find, after going to the dictionary, that this is an individual baking dish. Why must you bake individually?

Here's a tip: put it all in one big pan, and cut it up when everyone's at the table.

Mrs. Reagan, it seems that you could simplify things and save a lot of money. If you'd like to stop by for dinner some evening, I'll show you how it's done.

If you don't mind, everything will be on the same plate.

But it won't take us forever to wash the dishes.

the Reagan years

Out, Out, Damned Spot!

Summer of '98 faded into history, and the big bunch of people inched west over the bridges. The first oak leaf turned brown, the last rose of summer slipped silently to the ground and I found myself standing at the end of the Wychmere Harbor jetty, staring at September-blue water and struggling to find an answer to the question that plagues all of us:

If you had a dress with a big splootch on it, why would you keep it in your closet for a year and a-half?

And as a gull squawked and dropped a clamshell onto a nearby rock, I realized that I, too, have stains, and it's time to come clean about them.

I cannot—will not, in fact—deny it any longer. I am a spiller. I have spilled. And I ask forgiveness for my spills.

These aren't Big City stains. There are no political implications, and I'm pretty sure my telephone conversations about spilling have never been taped. Moreover, I don't own any dresses, and most of the people I hang around with don't even have offices, much less oval ones.

Mine are Cape Cod spots, and it doesn't take a team of

geneticists to figure out what they are and where they came from.

Last week there was something white and greenish—lobster and a gob of tamale, I'm guessing. (If you left that in your closet for 18 months, you'd probably have to move.)

The sticky brown of the week before was hot fudge from the Dairy Queen, and the non-sticky dark brown was composted cow manure that I've been working into the flower bed. The wet, non-sticky dark brown was from the dog's feet. After exploring the bog, she wanted to jump up and tell me what she'd seen.

Bloody streaks down my shirt and leg last month startled me. Finding no gaping wounds, I figured it out. Colonial Red Latex. I hope I got some on the house, too.

Purple stains are dangerously revealing. They tell the

world you are not grown up, that you had a grape popsicle at the beach and probably spent an hour or so chewing on the stick while reading a trashy novel and batting away yellow jackets.

Greasy fingerprints just below the neck of your t-shirt may be traced to that once-a-year-bag of salt and vinegar potato chips.

Scarlet dots mean you got laughing uncontrollably while drinking red wine with friends, and that nasty smear on the seat of your pants is proof that a seagull was at the far end of the Bass Hole boardwalk just before you sat down there to watch the sunset.

But I did not, repeat, did not, have a relationship with that bird.

We are what we spill. And if life contains wine and cow manure, dog paws, house paint and purple popsicles, it contains, too, soap and a washer and dryer.

But maybe some folks are attached to their spots. Maybe a spot is sort of a keepsake—a memento—a case of "the proof is in the pudding." So to speak.

Or perhaps—and this is a possibility—there is no dry cleaner in our Nation's Capitol.

the Clinton years

Under-The-Table Diplomacy

We sat around a table at Exford's White Horse Inn. I had finished a still-warm egg mayonnaise and was purring over my third ploughman's lunch in as many days. My friends were putting away golden portions of fried plaice, and we all kept stealing sidelong glances at the case filled with chocolate-loaded, fruit-layered, cream-slathered, nut-coated sweets—the calorie-crammed amen to an English meal.

I already had discovered, only 72 hours after touching down at Heathrow, that a village pub is the best place to while away any evening.

I had discovered that a ploughman's lunch, consisting of simple salad, a bit of pickle, sweet butter, a hunk of crusty bread and a fat wedge of Stilton cheese is one of the finest arrangements ever put on a plate and—despite its name—should not be bypassed as an evening meal.

And I was about to discover—in that pub surrounded by the sheep-dotted hills of Exmoor—the key to good international relations.

It was across the room, under a table, just to the right of four feet.

I chewed in slow motion and studied those feet. Two were of the extra-large sort, wearing box-like, no-frills

brown workshoes. The third and fourth were wrapped
in hosiery and tucked into sturdy, good-for-the-arches
black heels with laces.

I looked up then, into a pair of the best faces I'd seen
in awhile: cheery, clear-eyed and rosy-cheeked. The
man, as tall as his feet were long, looked like he could
pull a hay wagon if the horses were away for the day.
The chubby woman by his side chatted and chuckled
between bites of supper. Together, they were nearly as
appealing as my Stilton.

I looked under their table at what was, apparently, a
dropped scarf.

The scarf moved. It stretched and yawned and became
a Yorkshire terrier.

My friends and I, dog lovers of the highest order,
stopped eating long enough to take note of the animal's

good manners and to swap stories about how our own
dogs would behave, unleashed, in a public eating place.
Mine would carom from table to table, nosing around for
spillage, droppage and a free handout, all the while dis-
playing the just-orphaned, frequently-beaten and nearly-
starved look that cocker spaniels have perfected over
centuries.

But the four-legged scarf under the table stayed put,
half-wrapped around a chair leg.

The man and woman finished their meal and eased
back from the table. He loosened his belt. She patted her
mouth with a napkin and sighed.

One of my friends—the cruise director—couldn't
stand it any longer.

(We had taken on traveling duties according to personalities. Our driver adapted easily to staying on the left
and did not burst into tears when a tractor came straight
at us on a single-lane road. I, the navigator, was adept at
telling left from right, folding maps and giving directions
ahead of time—usually. Our cruise director sat in the
back seat, consulted guidebooks and provided historical
information from her extensive portable library. She was
assigned this job because she is curious, intelligent and
can read in the car without throwing up.)

That night, hoping not to be considered a rude or loud
American, she leaned toward the couple and said quietly, "My, you have a lovely dog."

It's doubtful that the lights went on all over England
at that moment. But they seemed to. The man and
woman rose as one and swept across the room to our
table, the scarf at their heels.

Pulling up chairs, smiling so broadly their eyes disappeared, they sat down and introduced us to "Thomas."

The farmer and his wife were down from the
Midlands for Bank Holiday weekend, so we all were
tourists in Exford. They had to bring Thomas along,
because the last time they left him at home he savaged

the two German shepherds so badly they required "stitching up."

We talked of farms and moors, of cities and country towns. We told them that not all Americans live in New York or Hollywood, and they told us they don't care much for Cher or Madonna. "They're joost up there singin' in their oonderwear," the man said, wide-eyed.

Thomas, who had heard it all before, draped himself over a big foot and fell asleep.

Much later, we walked out into the spring night, headed to our cars, wished each other well and said goodbye.

I was to learn, during my first stay in the West Country, that the English are daffy about their dogs, which is reason enough to be daffy about the English.

And two nights after meeting Thomas, I took a turn at international diplomacy.

We were down the road a few miles, having a pub supper at the Royal Oak in Winsford. Next to me, a man and woman sat beside each other. Lifting their forks in unison, looking neither left nor right, they ate in all-but-holy silence.

As was becoming my habit, I looked under the table. Stretched across the couple's feet was a huge mop of gray-and-white something-or-other. Two eyes blinked at me from what I had assumed was the back end.

I leaned toward my neighbors and said softly, "My, you have a lovely dog."

And the lights went on again all across England. Or so it seemed.

Her name was "Kim."

Passages

I Read the News Today, Oh, Boy...

Tuesday evening, a friend asked, "Well, are you devastated by this?" Heck, no. I'm getting tougher all the time. It takes more and more to make me sick to my stomach these days. Mine is the first generation to have the Wonderful World of Everything delivered straight to the house.

From the comfort of my living room, I've seen a President shot in a motorcade and watched a candidate dying on the kitchen floor of a Los Angeles hotel. I've seen the motel balcony where a civil rights leader was gunned down, watched same-day coverage of a war half-a-world away and stared at the remains of people who drank poisoned Kool-Aid on command. And that's only the top of the hit parade.

So, getting older by the minute, tougher by the newscast, I'm not devastated.

Just depressed.

But this event, for some odd reason, is a more personal affront. It has taken a nick out of me, and I don't think that's very nice.

"There are places I'll remember all my life,
Though some have changed,
Some forever, not for better,
Some have gone and some remain."

I still have all the tangible things: 19 albums, a dozen

or so books, old magazines, pictures in assorted sizes and a red felt banner that says what a lot of us said for a long time: "I love the Beatles." And, aside from those dust-collectors, I have two hundred songs in my head, ten thousand words on my mind and recollections of an almost-20-year association.

I did not grow up with the Beatles. I was pretty well there when they arrived on our scene. The four boys— just about my age—came spinning and whirling into my college dormitory by way of a 45 rpm record titled "I Want to Hold Your Hand." Another song came along. Then another. And by the end of the year, we were tuned-in ("turned-on" hadn't been invented yet), card-carrying followers.

Paul's melodies, some tripping, some puckish, others amazingly lovely, filled our heads and kept us humming. John's words gave us something else to hold. The boys matched our moods, sometimes created our moods and shared our fantasies, which, in those days, weren't so very odd.

If we felt mushy, there was a mushy Beatles song. A silly thing came along to be silly with, and there were reckless things to fill our daring days. And the boys were there, too, when our confidence slipped, when we twisted with doubts or wept with hurt.

> *"When I was younger, so much younger than today,*
> *I never needed anybody's help in any way.*
> *But now those days are gone, I'm not so self-assured.*
> *Now I find, I've changed my mind, I've opened up the door."*

I went to see the Beatles in concert, August 18, 1966, at Suffolk Downs. We were a tad old for the crowd, my friends and I, and were disgusted. All around us, little girls screamed themselves purple. They began dropping like flies. They fainted. They threw up. They were carried away by policemen who didn't understand.

Neither did we. We wanted to hear the music. What we got was an orgy, where a small, sweaty female thought if she shrieked "JOHHHHHHNN" loud enough and long enough, he would surely rush to her side and propose. (I, on the other hand, had pictured a quieter meeting, say, in a small café somewhere.)

We all grew up and away. I plodded along in my own direction, and the boys went anywhere and everywhere. We didn't share the drug thing, but still I loved their music. They left me behind again when they tripped off into meditation and George began playing a sitar, but the songs stayed with me. And because I felt like a longtime friend, I loved what they did best, tolerated what I didn't agree with and forgave them for being asses when they were asses.

Together, then separately, they stayed with the world and in mine. They were there for the joy of it and through the pain of it, and it seemed that they had an anthem for everything that faced us all.

"And when the night is cloudy
There is still a light that shines on me.
Shine until tomorrow,
Let it be."

So when John Lennon was shot Monday night, it took something out of me. A lot of people won't understand that. A lot will.

So heck, no. I'm not devastated.

People are killed very day.

Right?

Damn.

December 1980

47

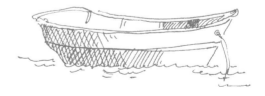

"Be Home for Supper"

My parents were totally irresponsible and didn't love me.

They couldn't have.

I mean, could they have?

First off, I didn't have a car seat. That is to say, I didn't have one of those things with straps that go around your waist and between your legs and under your fanny and across your chest. My car seat was—the whole back seat. I ricocheted from side to side, sometimes climbed over into the front to nestle between Mom and Dad, sat on the floor to play with the dog and occasionally stuck my head out the window when either he or I had to throw up. The throwing up (mine, not the dog's) stopped after my mother suggested I not sit looking out the window with my nose against the glass. When the world stopped flying past me sideways, my stomach settled down.

My parents didn't have those plugs to block electrical outlets. What they did was say to me, "Don't stick your fingers in the socket, or you'll get a shock."

So I didn't.

My parents didn't have those plastic tie-things that lock kitchen cabinets. What they did was say, "You can go into this cupboard, take out pans and use them for drums until the cows come home, but don't go into that cupboard because the soap and cleaning things in there are not good for you."

So I didn't.

My mother said, "Don't touch the stove when it's on, or you'll get burned."

So I didn't.

My folks didn't put poisons in out-of-the-way places, primarily because they didn't have anything that was poisonous—except canned stewed tomatoes, which I was sure would kill me.

My father never told me to not eat snow or suck on icicles, because he did both as a kid in Maine. So I did, too.

It's unlikely my parents warned me away from lead paint— although our home was probably slathered with it—because no one knew then that it was such nasty stuff. But they probably told me that gnawing on windowsills was not the best way to spend my time.

So I didn't.

Here's how much my parents didn't love me: they let me learn to ride a bike on a huge, red, dented, one-speed thing that had first belonged to my older brothers and sister. I slammed into a tree, got up, toppled over the curb and eventually wobbled off down the street to happiness and

freeeeeedom, bleeding from just two places on my knees.

Here's another mean thing my parents did: they made me talk to strangers. I was an absurdly shy P.K. (preacher's kid) in a church with about 300 parishioners, not one of whom I would speak to. So I learned to hold out my hand, smile and say, "Hello," "Yes, Please" and "Thank you." It was ugly.

In our New Hampshire summers, B.C.C. (Before Cape Cod), my folks waved me off early every morning, watching me climb into the back of our farmer neighbor's pickup truck to go off and "help him" (so I thought) deliver milk to the dairy and to folks along the way. I sat, or stood, bouncing up and down with every bump in the roads, and always came home in one piece—dusty, grinning and ready to go shovel up behind the cows.

And here's a really scary thing; we drank raw milk from that farm. When I ran down the hill to get bottles from the barn, it was still warm. It wasn't homogenized! It wasn't pasteurized! Didn't anybody CARE?! We could have died! Who knew where those cows had been?

After school most days, my friends and I would go home, leave our books, change our clothes, have a snack and then disappear to meet up with each other and do—whatever. Our parents never really knew where we were—only that we were with each other.

But every day, as I ran out, Mom said, "Be home for supper."

And I was.

Always.

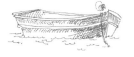

So Long, Pardner

Some of us are reaching the age and stage where the losses begin, and they sometimes come so close together that you're only halfway back up before you're down again.

But nobody ever told me that Roy Rogers would die. No one said that his going would make me feel like a six year-old again, aiming my cap pistol at anything that moved, tearing across the pasture with the wind in my hair and the imagined pounding of hooves beneath me. And when he left, I thought again of the two people who gave birth to a daughter but managed, with profound good humor, to tolerate my little buckaroo days.

It could hardly have been avoided. I had older brothers and a sister who was passionate about Roy Rogers and horses, and I was born into the cowboy generation and an all-boy neighborhood.

At the movies, in funny books and on television, we were surrounded by The Lone Ranger and Tonto, The Cisco Kid and Pancho, Range Rider, Wild Bill Hickok, Wyatt Earp and Lash LaRue.

We wrinkled our uppity little noses at Hopalong Cassidy and Gene Autry (while approving of their horses, Topper and Champion, however), because they looked old to us—more like middle-aged accountants than real cowboys, and no authentic cowboy would have been caught dead singing "Rudolph, the Red-Nosed Reindeer."

But Roy Rogers was—hands down—the King of our cowboys. First off, he was young and cute, with crinkly eyes and a shy smile. (The girl in me was very clear about that.) He wore snappy hats, sang great songs and nobody on earth ever had a more beautiful horse.

That singing business was no small thing in our family. When Roy and the Sons of the Pioneers began crooning "Cool Water," "Tumblin' Tumbleweeds" or "Blue Shadows on the Trail," we sang along with gusto and in as many parts as were on hand.

Roy was a good cowboy, a decent human and true-blue friend. In the neighborhood, we were not always any of those. Gabby Hayes would have called us "little whipper-snappers." We got rowdy now and then, and our favorite games involved ropes and pistols. "See Who Can Fall Dead the Best" was Number One, and on any given day passers-by might see a dungareed kid screaming, clutching his/her chest and taking a nosedive into the shrubbery.

In one effort to improve her child's social skills, my mother suggested (insisted) that I invite two little classmates over to play. Marilyn and Sandra arrived with dolls, and we went to my room. Marilyn and Sandra wanted to set up the card table and have a tea party. I wanted to throw them out the window.

That same window did me in sometime later. There was snow on the ground, as I remember. Mom was changing the sheets on my bed when she heard a noise behind the house. (Did I mention that we lived in the parsonage?) Looking out that damned window, she saw a small boy tied to a maple tree next to the clothesline. There was no one else around.

Mom ran down the stairs, tore into the yard and

sprung Warren, who was cold, soaked and sobbing his heart out. I'm fairly sure my mother had little or no experience with untying people, but she worked through a dozen or so of our most spectacular knots.

I can't recall what happened afterward.

However, I'd like to take this opportunity to say, "I'm sorry, Warren. Please don't try to find me."

During my cowgirl phase, I was deprived of just two things—real boots with pointy toes and heels and a two-gun holster set. I was spoiled beyond measure but not beyond propriety or safety. It's reasonable to assume that six-guns were not suitable attire for a minister's daughter who might have tried to wear them under her choir robe. And considering that within a three-year span I had twice fallen out of a hayloft, been trampled by a cow and gotten snarled in a bale of barbed wire, proper cowboy boots probably would have killed me. Instead, I got girly boots with rounded toes and flat heels—hardly the stuff of my dreams, but as close to the real thing as love, indulgence and practicality would allow.

And so, with one puny cap gun and faux boots, I rode the rails—which in this case had nothing to do with trains. Although I adored Trigger (as well as Silver, Scout, Tony, Champion, etc.), being on an actual horse was something of a problem. I was small and skinny, with neither the strength of body or character to manage something that was at least three times taller than I. So I rode the pasture fence. It was a good horse—willing, gentle and faithful to the end.

And there was an end—eventually. The gun and lasso got packed away. The boots wore out, and we moved far away from the fence. It's been years since I tied anyone to a tree, and I'm reasonably sure none of my old side-kicks wound up in the pokey. With any luck, we became people our hero would have liked.

Roy lingered on in us all. And as we grew up and

smarter, we learned his own life wasn't all campfires and close harmony, but had its hills and valleys, glory and grief. Just like ours.

He leaves behind his little buckaroos, getting older by the minute but never forgetting what the King of the Cowboys said to us so many times so long ago: "Goodbye, good luck, and may the good Lord take a likin' to you."

❖

All in the Same Boat

My friends and I are someplace we've never been before, and I think it would be a good idea for us to hold hands and stay together. And maybe whistle. And definitely talk—talk loud and long and scare away things that go bump in the Middle of Life.

Because that's where we are.

We just got here, and there's no map.

The winter of '90 brought deep snows and old friends to the back door—people who headed down here quietly, for their own off-season reasons. To find something. To get away from something. To reaffirm. Reestablish. Perhaps to locate a small piece of themselves they lost when they grew up, or maybe to find some kind of star to fix on—for now—for the duration.

A friend I had started singing with 27 years earlier sat cross-legged on the floor as we tuned long-ignored guitars and hunted for harmonies not-quite forgotten. I talked across breakfast with someone I had begun giggling with when we were very little. And one slate-gray evening, half-hidden behind a moustache at the kitchen door, was a smile I hadn't seen for 20 years.

These friends of mine don't know each other. That's the way it goes when you discover and save people along

57

the way—from here, there, school, work, childhood. They never meet or know how special they all are: intelligent, talented, sensitive, funny, loving, responsible—and entirely different from one another.

What they have in common is me, and what we have in common is abiding affection, shared history and the fact that we've fetched up here in the Middle of Life together.

The big chill of '90 saw long conversations over hot coffee, reminiscences over cooled wine. We swapped laughter, tears, anxiety, anger and some noteworthy cussing. And there was openness, the likes of which we'd not seen—or perhaps needed—before.

Across the coffee, around the confusion and with occasional anger stomping around in the background, I saw that my friends were having to be more sensible, more responsible and more loving than ever before in their lives. Some were caught and spun between the needs of their children and their parents.

We decided, with clarity that comes with being in the Middle of Life, that if friends in their twenties get together, they talk about what to do with their lives. In their thirties, they talk about what to do with their children. By forty, they begin to talk about what to do with their parents.

It's been said—much too often—that the grass is always greener next door. That was the issue facing one friend when her husband jumped the fence into another yard (a move, I suspect that had very little to do with grass), leaving her bewildered, angry and knocked flat by something she never saw coming.

The writer behind the moustache had given up a regular paycheck to try his hand at freelancing. This was a now-or-never leap of faith—in himself.

Another friend had decided that the move up to an important job in education would not be worth the built-in aggravation, and he was afraid that feeling that way made him a loser.

And down the road, someone else was roller-skating as fast as possible between children, an ill parent, the family-owned business and an ominous crack in the living room ceiling.

It seemed important to talk, to look for some reflection of ourselves in each other—explaining, asking, whistling together in the pitch black and wondering how we are to manage without safety nets.

When did we get to be the grownups?

The things that go bump in the Middle of Life aren't going away. They will, almost certainly, get scarier and we're afraid of them.

But maybe we're not as afraid of each other anymore.

Maybe the need to connect finally outwrestles the need to be self-sufficient.

The writer took lyrics from a song that meant something to him and set them above a story he wrote.

"Time it was, and what a time it was,
a time of innocence,
a time of confidences."

Most anyone who can identify those words without stopping to think is in the Middle of Life. And anyone located there knows that the lyricist was only half-right.

The innocence was then.

The confidences are now.

Why?

On the surface, two events of the past month are no more alike than mustard and roses. Many would be offended that I connect them in any way. That's their privilege.

But in the midst of sorrow that is touched with anger and shot through with confusion and a deep sense of loss, I see both events as a matter of life and death, of love and choices.

And I'm having trouble understanding.

Fourteen years ago, I brought home the only love money can buy—a tiny, black satin suggestion of what would become an intelligent, amusing, expressive and stubborn cocker spaniel named Samantha.

Sam and I took to each other immediately and, in a few short but messy months, resolved the only conflict we would ever have; she agreed to use the yard rather than the carpet.

From that point on, our relationship was based on mutual respect and compromise. Sam never learned how to balance a cookie on her nose, because both of us would have thought that stupid. But she knew what she had to know and, I suspect, a great deal more that she never told me.

She would come when called, if not otherwise occupied. If she was walking or thinking, eating, lying down, staring at a bird or watching a horse walk by, she would come when she damned well felt like it and not a minute sooner.

But early on, she decided that she would not chew the couch, bite, jump on people, run away, cross the road, bark unnecessarily or throw up in the car. I said I wouldn't, either, and we enjoyed a lifetime of love and friendship.

As Samantha neared her 15th birthday, things started to go wrong, and I began to worry. Her legs hurt, and something was the matter inside. She couldn't career around the yard, didn't want to play our old games and hadn't the gumption to wag her tail or do her supper-time dance routine.

She wasn't having a good time anymore.

She was sick and getting more so. I had to make a decision.

That decision hurt, because I loved her. But it had to be made—for the same reason. She'd had a lifetime of good health and good times. Those were gone. She'd had a lifetime of good care, and it was up to me to care for her just one more time.

I did. And Sam doesn't hurt anymore.

Several years ago, I met someone who was to become one of the best-loved people in my world. A person of considerable stature and exceptional talent, she enjoyed a life that was crowded with hard work, excitement, good friends, wonderful adventures, joy, love and humor. She was totally and enthusiastically plugged-in to life, and to know her was to receive some of that current.

I was wide-eyed with admiration, which she accepted

with quiet good humor, and she gave back support, encouragement and the gift of her friendship.

Some time ago, my friend received the worst of all pronouncements. She was ill, would become more so and no amount of positive thinking would alter the outcome.

And so she proceeded, in head-up fashion, her sense of humor taking over in the most unexpected places, at the most unimaginable times.

But the illness tore away her dignity and degraded the quality of that good life.

She wasn't having a good time anymore.

And the people who cared for her the most could only stand by, look on and wait.

It took a long time.

These two events have just taken place, and I'm left with the impression that we're permitted to show more compassion to a pet than to each other.

I'm having trouble understanding.

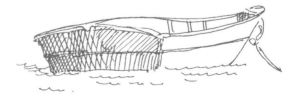

Key Issues

Not very long ago, I found a ring with eight keys hanging on a hook by the back door. Sitting at the kitchen table, I took the keys off the old ring, spread them out and studied them, one by one.

The result is this: I have not the remotest idea what any of those keys is for. They're not particularly old. There's not a skeleton key in the lot. Each one unlocked something or other in my life, but I don't know what, where, when or for how long.

When I was a teenager, I thought my brother had more keys than anyone in the world. They were on a huge clip that he fastened to his belt, and I marveled that the weighty contraption didn't yank down his pants.

But his was a life full of things that required keys. He owned an old inn with lots of rooms, as well as a 5 & 10 cent store that had front and back doors and a small safe with a lock. He had a car, drove a school bus, and was on the police force. And in his almost-nonexistent spare time, he sat at an old, oversized oak desk with two drawers that locked. There, in rare quiet moments, he fiddled with paper and pen and a square black typewriter, writing poems, song lyrics and stories—for himself, really—

spilling his thoughts and then locking them away.

My own first key (I didn't have a house key, because ours never was locked) was for an black Peugeot with a crank-open sunroof, on sale for $300 in Chatham. Dad wouldn't buy the car until he came back to Joe Baker's Garage here in town and made sure Joe could service a car with such a queer name. My father thought the only proper name for a vehicle was "Buick."

My first car, therefore, was one neither of us had ever heard of. The radio would come on only if I opened the glove compartment and then slammed it shut. I loved that old thing, the way everyone anywhere has ever loved a first car.

There have been keys to other cars, including a used

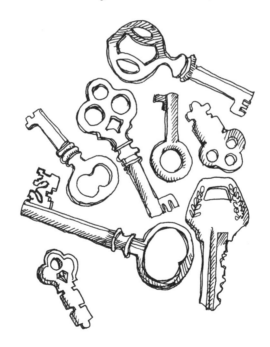

Chevrolet that had the first stereo radio with rear speakers. I was smitten. My father suggested that buying a car simply because I liked the radio was probably not the smartest way to shop, but I was deeply committed to those rear speakers. I've never forgotten how kind, supportive and restrained he was over the next few years, when everything on that car busted—except the radio.

My hand shook on the day I put a key into the lock of My Own House, only minutes after I had signed away my life for a 30-year mortgage, the monthly payment on which would be a staggering $173. But, having wised up a bit since the Chevy days, I never for a minute regretted buying that house key.

Over time, there have been keys to a Boston office, to a newspaper, to a summer theatre, to my sister's house and others. For many years, I had a key to our church. But Dad retired from the pulpit there, Mom took off her Choir Director's robe, and times changed.

Now, friends have left me keys to their summer homes, in case of winter emergencies. But the keychain I carry daily has gotten lighter. One for home/office. One for car.

Still, on the kitchen hook is a ring with eight keys. I don't know what they're for, but don't dare throw them out—just in case.

I'm all-but certain one of them might be to my parents' house. Maybe I couldn't quite manage to let it go.

Of all the keys in my life, that's the one I miss using most of all.

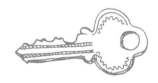

Cranky Yankee

The Spitting Image

Well, that just about does it. Time to pack away the ol' mitt and flip up the seats at Fenway. Sort of sad to see it end.

On the other hand, after 162 regular games, a league playoff series and The Big One, we've seen enough spitting to last a lifetime, thank you very much.

Baseball players have always spit, but never before has it been brought to us so up-close-and-personal—and in such glorious color. And you haven't lived until you've seen Bill Buckner let fly in Super Slow-Mo. Kind of plays havoc with the system if you're munching popcorn.

Assaulted by this rapid fire from April through October, you begin to identify and categorize the different styles of expectorating. Reggie Jackson, for example, shoots from between clenched teeth—in fits and starts— sort of like an oscillating lawn sprinkler—"zot, zot, zot!"

Then, too, you wonder about the source of the, ahh, liquid. There's tobacco, of course. But the other night, Darryl Strawberry chomped, spit, then blew a fat pink bubble. Wade Boggs appears to have a sweatsock packed in his left cheek. And we wonder if any of these guys have welcomed the recent return to the market of our personal childhood favorite—Blackjack gum—with its pungent licorice flavor that leaves your mouth filled with dark juice and tasting like a boot.

All of this leads to a bigger and deeper philosophical/sociological question that cannot be tossed aside lightly. Why, it must be asked, do only men spit? We have never seen a woman expectorate—on the street, out a car window or in a subway station. Little boys spit. Little girls do not.

Ask, too, why only baseball players spit. It may be argued that basketball players are too busy to do so, and they know that extra moisture on the court could be treacherous. Presumably, football players refrain from spitting because it might ricochet off their face masks.

May we assume that baseball players spit because they have nothing else to do? Because they have so much chewing time on their hands?

Hard to say. But if you want to avoid seeing frequent "zots," "whirps" and "pweets" on television, there are times when you must look away from the screen. When a player is hitting, running, pitching or catching, he will not spit. Before hitting and after hitting, before running and after running, prior to catching and after catching and both before and after pitching, he will spit.

So look away. (A side benefit here is that you may also avoid seeing Scratching or Adjusting.)

Maybe it's time to end the spit cycle. Maybe next year's Spring Training should include one more bit of discipline.

Or would that be too much to swallow?

Foot Notes

My sneakers died last week. I'd known for some time
that it was coming. They didn't look well. And I'd discovered that wearing them was the fastest way to clear a
room.

So I drove them straightaway to the dump, murmured
my goodbyes and headed to town for a new pair, having
learned that it's best to do these things quickly.

I found a sports shop selling footwear and went up to
a man selling footwear in the sports shop.

The conversation went quite a bit like this:

"Hi. Hot enough for ya?"

"Sure is. I'd like some sneakers."

"Huh?"

"Sneakers. Size 8. Medium. White."

"What?"

"White."

"Let me show you, ah, over here, what we have.
Running shoes. Fencing shoes. Windsurfing shoes.
Tennis shoes. Wrestling, racquetball, basketball and
squash. These over here are skydiving boots."

"Where are the sneakers?"

"Huh?"

"Sneakers. Size 8. Medium. White."

"What do you want to do with them?"

"Put them on my feet. I need two."

"I mean, what do you do *in* them?"

"Nothing."

"Ah, over here are running shoes and cross-trainers. Racing flats run from about $50 to $110. Training shoes, go, say, $40 to $85. Now, you want to consider flexibility, durability, the strength of the heel cup and the rear stabilizing lace that goes around the heel. You want a roomy toe box and a perforated insole at the ball of the foot."

"Actually, I want some sneakers with laces and room for my feet."

"Now this one has a Gore-tex upper. Clean it with denatured alcohol. The feature here is ballistic, bullet-proof nylon, which keeps your toenails from poking through the top."

"I keep mine pretty well cut back. They don't go anywhere."

"Check this sole here. It's fibram—very soft and highly flexible. Of course the price of these is dictated by where they come from—Korea, or Taiwan, from the Philippines or Yugoslavia."

"Do you have any from Brockton? White? Size 8?"

"Ha-ha. Brockton. That's funny. Now, over here are tennis shoes. This one has high density polyurethane in the part that hits the ground. Above that, for lightness, is a low density material. Look here. The three stripes down the sides—this isn't just a pretty shoe. These stripes give lateral stability. And also think about a straight last versus the curved last. There's a lot of discussion about that."

"I can imagine. See, I like to wear sneakers to the store or maybe to a movie. I like white, and I wear an 8."

"Do you run?"

"Well, I move pretty fast when I'm moving the lawn sprinkler. And I run to close the car windows when it rains."

"Do you pronate inward?"

"I beg your pardon?"

"Pronate. When you land, does your foot roll in? That's the varus aspect. The valgus aspect is when your foot rolls out. Some of these have heel cups to give medial support and help correct excessive pronation. This running shoe over here has an air bag inside. When you hit, the air compresses. It has little air cells trapped inside the sole. Now the tennis shoes are made for different surfaces. We have your clay court, your cement, your asphalt and your grass."

"Do you have hammock?"

"Huh?"

"Hammock surface. I like to wear my sneakers in the hammock."

"Are you kidding?"

"Yeah, I guess so. Here's my situation. I want some sneakers. Size 8. Medium. White. No stripes. No heel cup. No stabilizers and above all, no air bags. See, all your shoes here are for doing something. When I slide into my sneaks, I don't want to have to do something in them. I just want to yank them on and leave them there. They'll do whatever I do, but it won't be much. They'll just sort of go around with me. Understand?"

"Maybe you should check out the great colors we have here. Blue is the biggest seller, nationwide. Brown shades sell only in New England. Green is good, too. Great selection, huh?"

"Yup. It's really something. What's this over here—in the bin? Is this white? Hey! These are canvas, right? Not bad. How much?"

"$89.95."

Old School Ties

A classmate whose name didn't ring a bell and whose face I couldn't place called awhile back to ask if I'd signed up for our college reunion.

I said I would not be able to attend (already having made very firm plans to re-grout the bathtub that particular weekend—whenever it was).

"Oh, you should come," she said. "It's a great experience. The first night is pretty awkward, then things loosen up, and by the next night you've forgotten how old you are."

(Hmmmmm. How much grout will I need?)

She continued, in what I would describe as a "wheedling" tone. "A lot of single people will be there. Just about everyone's been married and divorced."

(Should I get white grout or something in a cream tone?)

"If you threw away the blue form, just take a little piece of paper and jot down what's happened to you since graduation."

(Jot? My life is a "jot?")

Finally, in a last-ditch effort to reestablish old ties, she

asked, "Are you still with that public relations company?"

"No," I said.

"Oh," she said.

"I left there in 1968," I said.

"Oh," she said.

(White grout. Definitely white.)

Flashdunce

My friend across the street has been dancing since she
was about a month old. She's tall, leggy, graceful—in
other words, someone I'd rather not be seen with in
public. She has all the moves. I can walk backwards—if I
pay attention.

Well, this friend has been pestering me to join the aerobics class she teaches. Pester, pester, pester. "You'll like
it," she says. "It'll make you feel good," she says. "Try
it," she goes on.

A few weeks ago, being weak-minded as well as weak-
muscled, I agreed to go—once.

So my friend—after warning me to never eat broccoli
before an exercise class—showed up at the door wearing
this get-up from Star Trek: glow-in-the-dark pink leg
thingies that didn't stop where her legs do—a "unitard,"
she called it—with mini-briefs pulled over, and little
cuffed socklets with snow-white "aerobics shoes."

I don't have a "unitard" or socklets. So I wore my bare
legs, with some baggy white shorts, a t-shirt that says,
"Oh, no, I forgot to have children!" and sneakers with
grass stains on them.

We drove to the studio.

Other people arrived. "Hi," "Hi," "Hi," everybody said
to everybody else. There were blue tights and purply

ones, pairs of socklets and shiny leotards and unitards. Two people brought their own privately-owned personal floor mats. (I have a chair pad in the shed, but it's got mildew on it and smells.)

My friend, snow-white-sneakered toes pointing out, glided to the front of the room, snapped a CD into the machine and hollered, "Let's go, girls!" The music exploded, and she swished her arms up over her head. Swish, swish, swish—everyone else did the same.

I wasn't ready, so my swish was late.

I had figured I would do this only if I could hide at the back of the room. But at the back of the room there was no hiding place, because the front of the room was mirrored. Wall-to-wall. Everyone could see every part of everyone else—every lump and bump—every front and behind—and some of us were behinder than others.

It began. First were these stretching exercises designed to yank and loosen thighs, arms, stomach, neck, calves, feet. The whole body-beautiful, and I use the term loosely. Down on this leg and push the other one back. Twist this arm and touch a knee with the opposite elbow. Flex toes and stretch them. Heave and thrust and pull and hold and one-and-two-and-three-and-four-and-one-and-two-and-do-eight-more!

Limbs were flying. These people knew what they were doing.

I didn't.

I was getting mixed up about what year it was, and I couldn't come up with the name of the President of the United States. I was doing left-right instead of right-left, bouncing on the wrong foot and flexing instead of pointing.

Every part of me was slopping up and down, and my nose began to throb. I needed oxygen, and we were still in the warmup phase. Only 55 minutes to go.

I'd never made a will. Who would give my dog a good

home? One-and-two-and-kick-and-twist-and-crouch-and-stretch-and-keep-it-up!

One of us in the room was having a swell time. Up front, the instructor (note the word "friend" is no longer in use) took frequent breaks to double over, screech and point at me. Having a bare-legged hippopotamus in the back row had made her day.

I resorted to biting sarcasm. When she said, "Now we'll do 30 pushups," I said, "In a pig's eye." When she'd yell, "Get that leg higher," I'd yell back, "Oh yeah?" or something clever like that.

The music pounded. The beat went on. The windows steamed up. The others began 10 minutes of running in place, and I paused to press my brow against a cool pipe. Then everyone did some cooling-down routines, wiggled their heads, shook their legs, arched their backs, put on their coats, said "Bye-bye" and went home.

The instructor gave me a pat on the back and a small plastic bag of Epsom Salts.

She suggested I take a hot bath.

I suggested she swallow her unitard.

She smiled. "But don't you feel good? Wasn't it fun? Tell the truth."

The truth was, I had been hurt, laughed at, humiliated and bruised—in both body and spirit.

But I have to go back.

Somebody gave me tights.

And socklets.

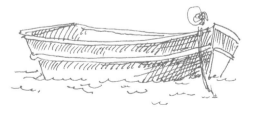

❖

Position is Everything

The letter came last Tuesday—and not a moment too soon.

I was feeling chunky and poor. The house trim was flaking, every window was cloudy with a winter's worth of goop and I had just discovered that the adage "As ye sow, so shall ye reap" has nothing to do with my back yard. I had sowed grass seed and reaped dandelions. Worst of all, I had just finished stuffing five extra pounds of me into last year's shorts.

So I waddled through the dandelions to the mailbox and found The Letter.

It was from American Express, and American Express thinks I'm practically perfect in every way.

"In today's competitive world," the letter began, "it is meaningful—as well as personally gratifying—to be awarded special recognition. So you'll undoubtedly be pleased to learn that you've attained what American Express calls 'Preferred Status'—an accomplishment for which you should feel justly proud."

(I do! I do!)

"It means that because of the position you've attained in life, we're confident you will be accepted for card-membership.... And since you are among our most desirable prospects, we are prepared to offer you privileged consideration when you apply."

(This is so exciting.)

"You see, American Express imposes no pre-set spending limit. Purchases are approved based on your ability to pay as demonstrated by your past spending, payment patterns and personal resources."

(Uh-oh.)

"The Card is the perfect complement to your lifestyle. Use it in hotels, resorts, fine stores and restaurants of quality."

(Even Chicken-on-a-Stick?)

"Because of your excellent reputation, you've earned Preferred Status. It's a privilege we're proud to offer...a sign you've earned our respect and trust. Do fill out the streamlined application today and experience the preferred treatment you deserve."

I skipped happily back through the beautiful dandelions, feeling thin and preferred. "I'll do it," I thought. "I'll use it to take a cruise—or to hire a dandelion-plucker—or someone to paint the trim—or someone to let out my shorts. It's only $35 a year."

I thought some more. "I can charge it on my VISA card."

TV, or Not TV

Dear Boss of Television,

Not to be rude or anything, but what are you people doing? I mean, what are you doing?

Here we sit with 400 channels, and all but, say, three of them show nothing but poo.

In your world of demographics, I belong in the "I Love Lucy," "Howdy Doody" and "The Mouseketeers" category. But here's some information for you: there are a lot of us out here who aren't too interested in ugly families, crime scene investigations, serial killers, or made-for-television movies about child molestation.

We get all that in the newspaper.

And what on earth makes you think that having a bunch of women try to win a date with a phony millionaire, or making teams of people eat worms on an island, or sending some fairly dumb folks off to travel all over creation to win a race has anything to do with "reality?"

If nobody who works for you can think of anything to actually write these days, leaving you with nothing but "reality" shows, here are a few suggestions:

How about something where people line up at the Registry of Motor Vehicles? Whoever gets to the head of the line first and isn't then told he's in the wrong line wins a new license plate.

And here's a "reality show" for you. Have a bunch of elderly people park in those convenient handicapped spaces at the supermarket. Then see how many of them collapse before getting to where the milk, bread and eggs are.

Oh, and just one more. It's cute. People with whopping electric bills invite representatives of the company to come over and tell them why their bills are so high. This one is lots of fun, because it's a guessing game. The homeowner says to the electric man, "Is it my refrigera-

tor?" The man looks at a chart and says "No." The homeowner asks, "Is it all my lamps?" The man says "No." "Is it my window fan?" "No." See, there's a twist at the end. The first homeowner to say, "I give up!" wins. You could call this show "Heads, We Win; Tails, You Lose."

While I'm talking to you, Mr. Boss, have you people lost all the Christmas season movies? Have you thrown away everything that might make us feel warm and content and hopeful and friendly toward one another?

I notice there is no shortage of films suitable for, say, Hallowe'en. The TV listings for the last week of October include the following: "The Glow," "Madhouse," "Don't Look Under the Bed," "Eight-Legged Freaks," "Bang, Bang, You're Dead," "The Frighteners," "Nightmare on Elm Street," "Hallowe'en" (I through V) and "Friday, the 13th" (I through VIII!).

Do you have gas or something? Aren't you happy? Don't you want anyone else to be happy? Is the real world not scary enough for you? If a child gets kidnapped one week, is there a rule that you must make a movie about it the next week? If a man beats his wife to death with a hammer, how long does it actually take you to buy the film rights?

And just one more thing. What's the story with commercials? Are those ad people on Madison Avenue doing drugs?

I won't belabor this, but car commercials puzzle me. Somebody's driving at 90 miles an hour through the desert or bouncing over boulders on the way up a mountain. Nobody says anything, and nobody tells us what car it is—until the very end. You know what? That's too late. Nobody remembers, and nobody gives a poop. Why not put the name of the car at the beginning? And how about a commercial where someone drives within the speed limit, maybe on a normal road with potholes, maybe slowing to avoid a turtle or wave to a neighbor.

I can't buy a car if it only works going 90 on the Bonneville Salt Flats. I need something I can drive to the dump and the library.

Finally, I'd like to ask about those commercials for medicine. What's up with that whole thing? We see people walking along the beach or sitting on the porch—sometimes playing catch in slow motion—whatever. One of them may be limping—or holding his head. Then somebody says in a loud voice, "Ploovitex could improve your life." Then somebody else sort of whispers the bad stuff about Ploovitex. (Shhhh.) "Ploovitex should not be taken by women who are pregnant or nursing or thinking about becoming pregnant or nursing, by children under six, by anyone suffering from asthma, constipation, high blood pressure or fear of spiders. Possible side effects are minor and may include stroke, seizure, irregular heartbeat, difficulty breathing, nausea, vomiting or diarrhea."

Then the louder voice comes back. "Ask your doctor if Ploovitex is right for you."

Well, how do I know? What's it for? Nobody says. And if seizure and stroke are your notion of "minor" side effects, what are "major" ones?

That's all I wanted to say, Mr. Boss of Television. I think you're doing a stinky job—whoever you are.

Plastic Fantastic

It was pathetic. Worse than that. Embarrassing. I had been invited to attend one of the established sociological and cultural events of the 20th century, and what happened? I failed—miserably and completely.

I didn't order one single piece of Tupperware.

It all began with a postcard invitation from a friend who was to be the hostess of a party. I was urged to bring another friend and win a prize.

My first thought was to leave town or, perhaps, to break a leg in two places. I had mind-pictures of sitting on a too-small, straightback chair in an over-warm living room, listening to scads of bowls being burped to lock in freshness.

But then the clincher. The note said that my friend would earn extra points if I would just show up. That's all. Just be there.

So I went, ready to learn everything there was to know about food storage.

I was a first-timer, and it showed. I didn't know what to do or how to act. The room was filled with hard-core users. Some people had tiny Tupperware bowls on their key chains. They knew the catalogue codes, they knew the colors, they knew the drill.

As the room got really hot, the selling began. Products were held up, handed around, described, praised and demonstrated. They burped and popped and sealed. They came apart and snapped back together. Everyone laughed and chatted and ate and had some special punch that tasted extra good and made everyone giggle louder.

The Tupperware lady told how you could put stuff in this one and serve things in that one, how you could stack and pack and whack it without breaking it.

The pros in the room said "Amen!" to this and "That's right!" to that as they compared experiences with the various useful doodads.

Then the woman told us she had made some tuna salad that stayed fresh for two weeks in this little burped bowl. And I believed, yes, I believed, although I felt certain I would never get within a mile of two-week-old tuna and mayo.

Then the ordering began, and I turned clammy.

Flipping through the catalogue, I hunted for something to buy—to help my friend win an electric mixer.

A sturdy container that separates pickles from brine? I don't need that. I just reach into the jar, lift a pickle and shake it.

A good tough set of bowls for storage of leftovers? As a rule, I don't have leftovers. If anything's left on my plate, I usually store it in the dog. (She burps, too.)

Other people were scribbling away, ordering, adding up, planning the next party.

I slumped in my straightback chair. I couldn't do it. If I ordered a bacon container, I would have to buy bacon. If I got a cake-taker, I'd have to make a cake and take it someplace.

Slinking off into the night, feeling like a failure, I hoped that no one I knew would ever have a lingerie party.

Mail Call

Dear AT&T,

My recent bill included an 11 cent charge for your "Universal Connectivity Fee." As I have no interest in being connected to the universe, I have deducted the 11 cents.

Dear Pharmacist,

I picked up my dog's prescription today, the one that says "Monbleau, Holly, dog" on your label. That label also says, "To be taken by mouth. Do not drink alcohol while taking this medicine. May cause drowsiness. Do not take while driving or while using machinery." Just want you to know that I read her the instructions, and she says "OK."

Dear Verizon, NStar and KeySpan,

Who are you? Did you used to be New England Telephone, Old Colony Gas Company and Cape & Vineyard Electric? I'm just asking, because I don't know which bill is what anymore. And who did Comcast used to be?

Dear Kellogg's,

It's very clever of you to have child-proof packaging for your cold cereal. It would be simply awful if children had access to Rice Krispies without adult supervision. But that inner wrapping seems to be adult-proof, too. I tussled with a new box of cereal this morning, the plastic stuff finally let go, and now there are raisins all over the kitchen.

Dear Black & Decker,

Your new toaster works very well. I read the directions and noticed the following statement: "Do not use under water." I'm curious about this, because the directions for my new hair dryer said the same thing. Has there been a problem with people drying their hair and making toast under water?

Dear Ms. Adams,

Thanks very much for your letter, but I am very happy with my current mortgage rate, and, no, I don't have credit problems that you could help me solve. Everything's fine, but I'm wondering about one thing; below your signature—why did you write "Se Habla Espanol?"

Dear NASA,

If I understand correctly, you folks built a golf cart-size rover that has wheels, a robotic arm and cameras. You packaged it in gigantic bubble wrap and sent it into space. It spent more than six months traveling 35 million miles, landed on Mars, unwrapped itself, rolled off its pad and started working.

Could one of your people please stop by here and take a look at my vacuum cleaner?

Local Color

❖

Main Street

Judge Gershom Hall kept an eye on Main Street from his second-floor office in the old Eldredge Building. In his pocket he carried a roll of bills that would choke a horse, or so I heard. And that's all I ever knew about him. I saw him now and again when I was small, but never met him.

When he died several years ago, my brother wrote a letter to the editor, recalling a day in 1959.

My brother died in 1987, and Judge Hall's son, Robert, died last year. Anyone who knew Bob will remember that he kept everything, and in the clearing out of his law office, someone found that letter and gave me a copy.

I'm tucking it in here—for David—and for those who remember our Main Street—or their own.

Dear Sir:

July, 1959. I had been assigned to Harwich Port by Police Chief George Baldwin. My duties were to direct traffic on Route 28 (Main Street), from South Street to Bank Street.

This particular day was typical, except for one incident; I asked Judge Hall to move his car off his own land.

Minnie had relieved Gladys on schedule at Wattie B's, and Frank Thompson had picked up his paper there, leaving his car with the door open and the motor running. Alice Small had driven Ed to the watch shop on Sea Street, had spent some time reading with him and then left for East Harwich. Fred Young and Joe Baker were dispensing gas and directions, and some of Mildred Fonda's antiques had been placed on the front lawn at her shop. Bill Hurst, John Caplice, Chet Robinson, "Papa" Vagenas, Sid Moody—their shops all were open.

My daughters rocked in unison on the side porch at Kemah Lodge. The front porch was reserved for guests.

As the sun moved, Marie Morgan lowered the awnings, and Fred Boscheinan took his post beneath them. Sue Gorham walked up to Cape Cod Five, "Pop" Hansen was building sandwiches, Dutch's Barber Shop and the market were doing business as usual and Beatrice Martin was taking her daily stroll up Main Street.

I had waved Alvin and Roy Eldredge out of Sea Street, crossed Route 28 with Eva Bassett and chatted with Helen D'Elia on her way home from the A&P. Howard Ellis stood on the steps of the movie theater. (I was to cover the matinee, and Barney Taylor would be on duty for the evening show.)

And so went this day.

When the car drove onto the sidewalk in front of the Eldredge Block, I thought, "This is a real wiseguy." I confronted the driver when he came back to his car. He explained that the sidewalk was double depth, was private property, not owned by the state or town and was, in fact, owned by him. He told me his name was Gershom Hall. I said I was pleased to meet him, and suggested that he was setting a bad example.

To the best of my recollection, he never parked there again.

Late that night, I rocked on the porch. The lights in The New Yorker Restaurant went out. I called "Goodnight" to Denise and Roselle as they turned into the Schoolhouse lot for home.

Then a car pulled out from behind the Eldredge Block and headed slowly west. "Goodnight, Dave." Gersh Hall lifted his hand from the wheel as he spoke. "Goodnight, Gersh," I called, as I got up to go inside.

Harwich Port was closed for the night.

David H. Monbleau

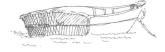

❖

A Cape Cod Conundrum

Bumpy Eldredge went missing on a Tuesday in the wet part of spring.

But maybe I'd better back up here, so you know who this is and what it's all about.

Bumpy Eldredge was, to be accurate, Bumpy Two. His father, Bumpy One, was the son of Vernal Eldredge and the former Ella Chase, that couple having come to the Cape from downeast Maine sometime around 1890. They built a house in Hooksham and proceeded to have six children, Bumpy One being the first.

Vernal went to fishing and building. Bumpy One followed his father to fishing, got sick over the side every time out and so settled down to building.

You're probably wanting to ask what Bumpy's real name was, but you needn't bother. I don't know, and I can't remember anyone ever saying.

At any rate, Bumpy One married Sylvanus Doane's second daughter, Louise, and they bought a house two doors back from the Legion Hall, across the street from the Rogers' place. That doesn't really matter, because the

Rogers have nothing to do with this so I won't mention them again.

Anyway, Bumpy One and Louise had Bumpy Two. From now on, I'll call him just Bumpy, because his father was long gone by the time this happened. Good thing, too.

Maybe here's a good place to tell you about the town, so you get some idea of what was what and where was where.

Hooksham (that's said Hook-sham) was just a regular town furnished with all the necessaries. On the main street was a church for every inclination, a hardware store, one place that sold clothes and notions, two gas stations and a 5 & 10 cent store that had a fountain and 14 silver-colored stools with leatherette seats of a sort of medium brown. (Cokes were a nickel, hotdogs 25 cents and frappes were not the same as milkshakes.) Down the road was a movie theater, and up past the old Esso station there was a store that sold fruit, vegetables, live bait and taxi rides.

A few blocks east of the movie house was a big wooden hotel. Folks—most of them on the old side—stayed there nearly all summer. Every evening—after an early supper—they'd stroll up the street to see what was or wasn't happening. Along the way, people with porches would sit and rock and watch the hotel folks walk by. All this walking and rocking made for good entertainment in the summertime. Young people lined up waiting for the movie or snuck around behind the newspaper store to smoke and choke.

There were 1,000 people in Hooksham, 6,200 in the summer, when people from away came down, unstuck their windows, aired mattresses, beat winter dust out of scatter rugs and got down to the serious business of doing almost nothing until Labor Day. Then they'd lock windows, close shutters, put on their shoes and leave, to the great relief of local people who had had just about enough of them for the time being.

Everyone would be glad to see everyone else again the next summer, but for now the town settled into itself and folks listened to leaves fall.

Bumpy Eldredge grew up in this town that was quiet sometimes and noisy other times, and he took after his father when it came to work. Bumpy could turn his hand to anything: mend a fence, patch a roof, paint a house, add a room, repair wiring, replace a furnace— whatever was needed—like many a Cape Codder, before or since.

His father gave him just three pieces of advice. He said, "Show up when you say you will, set a fair price and stick at the job 'til you finish." Bumpy took that advice and ran with it.

And the more he ran, well, the more he ran, if you catch my drift.

He'd take one job, then another, and another. Before long, he was as busy as a one-armed paper-hanger. (I forgot to tell you he could also hang wallpaper.)

After awhile, it got so he would start a job just a little bit before he finished the previous one. Then he'd take some money for a third job before he'd done everything on the second one.

Now, Bumpy was a nice appearing man with a quick smile. Folks liked him and knew he was good at what he did. So they hired him—and then waited. And waited some more.

I remember when the Amos Walkers needed new windows all around the house. The weights were gone in the old ones, and they were leaking and rattling something wicked. Bumpy gave a good price for the job, got the windows and piled up boxes of them in the side yard. Well, when it was right onto hurricane season, those windows were still in the boxes, where they were not likely to do much good.

One winter several years back, Eulalie Symmes had to spend three nights at her daughter's because Bumpy didn't come back when he said he would to replace the oil burner motor. She near froze. And that time he didn't come back to finish building and capping the Stewarts' new chimney? A raccoon came down it into the living room and—well—I don't even want to tell you what that place looked like the next day.

There probably are fifty or so more stories like that, but you get the idea.

The situation went from bad to worse, and everybody knew there would be trouble sooner or later when Bumpy went to the hardware store and bought twelve ladders.

What he did was this: he'd start a job and put a ladder against the house, or the garage, or on the front lawn. Then he'd go off on another job but leave the ladder at the first place.

So the folks there would say, "He'll be back pretty soon. He's left his ladder here."

Before long, there were ladders all over town. And people kept saying, "He'll be back. He left his ladder."

Now that you know what'd been going on, I can go back to where I started.

Bumpy Eldredge went missing on a Tuesday in the wet part of spring.

His ladders were all over the place, but he was not to be found.

People figured he'd gone to his lake camp down Maine, but folks there hadn't seen hide nor hair of him.

Then one weekend, the Clarks came up from New York to open their summer place, and they saw Bumpy's pickup around back of the house. The bulkhead was open, so they figured he'd come to put in the new furnace he'd promised them in October of the previous year.

The bulkhead led to an old Cape Cod cellar, which, if you don't know, is a small place—quite often round—just big enough for a furnace, some mice and a family of daddy long-legs.

Douglas Clark walked to the bulkhead, yelling, "Hey, Bumpy!"

There was no answer. Douglas saw a pair of boots—or, I should say, the soles of a pair of boots—at the top of the stairs.

Well, the boots were attached to Bumpy, and he was not replacing the furnace.

He was as cold as a dead haddock. In fact, he was as dead as a dead haddock.

The police chief said he'd been hit over the head with

a big piece of wood. Looked like it came from a ladder, he said.

Douglas Clark found those boots and their owner in the old round cellar a few years ago now.

And it sure is a conundrum, because to this day nobody knows what happened to Bumpy Eldredge.

He had a quick smile, clever hands and a dozen ladders, so you might wonder, "Who would kill him?"

'Course, the question folks around here are asking is, "Who wouldn't?"

Summer Friends

If I close my eyes and let that summer's end feeling wash over, I can see us there again—sitting close together on the beach, laughing wildly, talking quietly—or not talking at all. Being eleven, then thirteen, then sixteen. Growing year-by-year, but staying the same with each other.

That summer's end sensation— a sweet, sad recollection—is felt only by those who live in a place where people come and go, because some of our best friends came and went with the season.

The kids funneled in from around the country, reopening family homes and summer friendships. My own warm-weather cronies arrived on schedule in June, July or August, from Washington, D.C., Tennessee, Pennsylvania.... We'd reunite tentatively, hesitantly, tiptoeing around one another for all of a day before slipping into our old easiness.

Reclaiming our space by the lifeguard stand at Bank Street Beach, reestablishing ownership of the back booth at Cape Cod Pharmacy, we settled into summer—more sure of each other than we were of ourselves in those puzzling, stumbling years.

By today's measure, we were an ordinary, dull,

unimaginative little band. We had no boats, no cars, little money and never gave much thought to any of the three. We met daily at the beach, dined occasionally on Pop Hansen's mammoth sandwiches, walked to the movies (and sometimes collected for the Jimmy Fund there), hiked to the Dairy Queen and went regularly to the Wednesday night dances at Pilgrim Church. Older siblings gave us rides to the late, lamented Storyville to see The Kingston Trio, The Limelighters.... We screamed and jumped out at each other from behind bushes after seeing "Psycho" together.

We spent very little time at my house, his house, her house or their house. Where we were, usually, was "out" in our own, shared, neutral territory.

What we had most was each other, and that was enough. We knew next to nothing about one another's winter lives and didn't care. There was no time but the present. There was nothing but summer.

August was much shorter than July. Every year it disappeared while we weren't paying attention, and dead ahead was the dreaded leave-taking.

They were going. I was staying, and that was the heavier burden. On Labor Day my whole world went over The Bridge.

We got older. The pattern changed. She started chambermaiding. He worked in the laundry. I was a soda jerk, and the beach was a sometime thing.

One of those years, we knew life had changed and that most of us would not see each other again.

And that's what happened.

But I still get that summer's end feeling. And if I close my eyes, I see us again. Close together.

I hope they remember.

106

Sounds of Silence

Some friends from New York came up for a weekend summer before last and fussed about not sleeping well the first night. It was too quiet, they said.

I imagine they were used to their own lullaby of Broadway: horns and sirens and squealing brakes—and maybe a scream or two. They missed those things. Well, and who wouldn't.

Last summer, I drove against the grain—and the traffic—and headed for Maine to spend a few days with an Ohio friend who'd rented an old cottage on a lake there. Leaving Cape Cod in July was a heady experience; I half-expected some kind of police to stop my car at the bridge and send me home.

But nobody did, and I drove six hours to a town with a year-round population of four hundred, one intersection and a store that sold ten or twelve items and had a huge wheel of cheddar cheese. You had to drive twenty minutes to get any substantial groceries. But not cheese.

The point is, that place was quiet. The cottage was on a fire road off the main "highway," and I use the term while chuckling. Every time we drove up the fire road to the "highway," I stopped and looked left and right before pulling out into traffic. We must have gone up that fire road ten times, and not once was there a car coming along the main road in either direction—as far as the eye could see.

That's quiet.

At night, silence came down like a garage door, and we rocked on the porch, looking out at the lake, listening to nothing—the most nothing I've ever heard. Perfect and total silence, until—

"I heard loons on the lake last night," my friend said. We rocked.

"They sound like cows," she said.

"What? No, they don't," I said, stopping my rocker and thinking she must be off hers.

"Yeah, they do. Listen. Did you hear that? A loon."

"That's not a loon."

"What is it? A cow?"

"A bullfrog."

"Are you sure?"

"Very."

Apparently my friend is nature-challenged. That's all right. She knows more about the Middle East than I do.

Then—across the water—a fluting, fluttering, lonely cry.

"That's a loon," I said, grateful for the sound, content to have driven six hours to hear it.

More silence. Absolute. With only the weeping of a loon and the "ga-lunk" of the bullfrog.

This is a roundabout way of saying that Cape Cod isn't all that quiet. We have four seasons here by the bog, three of them noisy: peepers, bullfrogs, crickets and winter.

Peepers are little tree frogs. Oldtimers called them "pinkwinks" and "peewinks." Whatever the name, the sound is the same, as they fill the bog—

holding onto branches—or perhaps each other—and making the happiest possible racket—an evening ode to spring. Even if it's snowing, spring is here. Peepers don't lie. The world is a better place with pinkwinks in the yard.

In early summer, peepers pipe down and the "cows" take over. Bullfrogs you can't see—bullfrogs by the dozens, maybe by the thousands—provide the nighttime concert, performing their own Anvil Chorus at top volume. "Ga-lunk. Ga-lunk!"

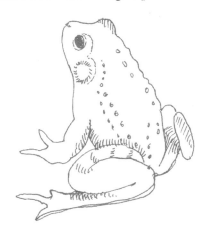

Creature by creature, the nights pass, and in late August, with the sounds of pinkwinks and frogs a fond memory, another tribe moves into town—and often into the house.

The song to summer's end is performed by crickets—crickets in the bog, crickets in the bushes—crickets on the hearth—crickets behind the couch.

So I don't understand what those New York people were talking about.

I think it gets pretty noisy around here.

Listen sometime.

Other books by the author:

Comments from readers about
The Inevitable Guest

It's wonderful! It's true, it's funny and it's environmentally friendly. Genuine laughter is so rare. You have scored!
Falmouth

"I wish you well in your efforts to write a new book. I would like to purchase a copy—especially if it will make me smile like The Inevitable Guest *did."*
Ohio

"A book that makes people laugh out loud."
Centerville

"I was given a copy for Christmas, and once I started reading and laughing, I could not put it down."
Weston

110

❖

"One of the funniest, most endearingly witty books I have ever read. I laughed out loud and had tears in my eyes."
Springfield

"Please send six copies to our home in Hyannis Port. We are living in London for awhile, but the Cape is where our hearts and guest rooms are."
England

"I expected one big joke, but as I read, I realized this is non-fiction! You've pulled off a great sleight of hand by being a neutral observer with a sense of humor."
Harwich

"I'm going to be very blatant and put it on the guest room night table!"
Florida

Marcia J. Monbleau has been a Cape Cod resident most of her life. She spent 17 years as a newspaper reporter and Feature Editor, was Publicity Director at the Cape Playhouse in Dennis for seven years, and for 10 years was host and executive producer of "Offstage," a local television program featuring chats with Playhouse stars. Her first play, *oldfriends.com*, was produced in 2002 at the Cape Playhouse and at New York's Queens Theatre in the Park. In the past several years, the author has become a popular public speaker, both on and off-Cape. She lives in Harwich Port, next to an old, unfarmed cranberry bog that is fast-becoming a forest and home to all creatures small and smaller.

Lucretia Romey is a widely-traveled artist and illustrator who now lives in an old family home in East Orleans on Cape Cod. She has published numerous pages of sketches in newspapers on the Cape and in northern New York, and her illustrations have appeared in many books. She has been one of the primary illustrators of shipboard logs while teaching on dozens of cruises over the past 10 years. She also is an award-winning quilter and her work is in various collections, including the American Quilt Museum in Padukah, Kentucky. Her watercolors have been exhibited in New York City at the American Watercolor Society and at other shows.